To anyone who think they can't do it,
YOU CAN!
never give up and always have faith
that you can,
because God will move mountains.

Micah and his grandpa John
always play basketball
together every day after school.

Micah and his best friend, Isaac, walked to school every day, talking about trying out for the school basketball team.

As soon as Micah and Isaac got to school, they immediately talked to the basketball coach about trying out for the team.

After school, Micah and his grandpa practiced basketball for hours and hours that day, like they always do.

Later that day,
Grandpa told Micah
to get ready for dinner.

As Micah sat down at the dinner table, he told his grandpa about trying out for the basketball team. Grandpa got so excited for Micah.

Grandpa John immediately grabbed his Bible and read to him, "For truly, I tell you, if you have faith the size of a mustard seed, you will say to this mountain, 'Move from here to there,' and it will move; and nothing will be impossible for you." (Matthew 17:20-21).

Micah begins to say,
"So all the faith I need is as
small as a mustard seed?"

Grandpa john had the biggest
smile and walked Micah to bed.

Micah said his prayers before he went to bed and was excited praying to god about his basketball tryouts tomorrow.

Micah woke up the next morning so excited. He even brought his bible to school and shared the verse he learned with grandpa to his best friends.

Later on that day at school,
basketball tryouts were about
to begin. Micah was so excited
to show the coaches
what he could do.

Tryouts were starting and Micah saw Issac outside the gym upset. Micah began to ask "what's wrong" he replied, I'm scared I won't make the team. I just want to give up.

Micah ran to the locker room and showed his best friend the verse him and his grandpa knew. Micah replied, "all you need is faith as a mustard seed and God can move mountains. You can and you will make the team with god on your side Issac"

Issac began to smile and gave
micah the biggest smile.
Issac replied, you're right Micah.
Lets pray and show these coaches
what we got!

The next day Micah and Issac
went to the school to see
if they made the team.

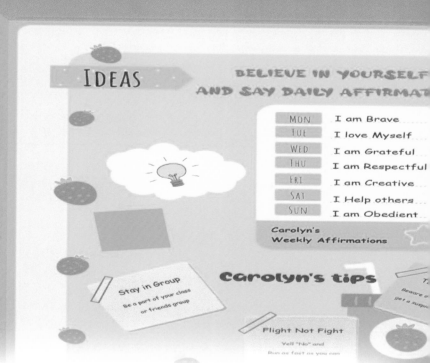

They looked at the list and both Micah and Issac were excited to see their names on the list for the basketball team. Issac looks at Micah and says "We can and WE will with god on our side".

Made in the USA
Columbia, SC
28 July 2024

38942259R00020